W9-AQL-328

BURT FRANKLIN: RESEARCH & SOURCE WORKS SERIES 573
Theatre & Drama Series 12

BUNKER-HILL

NEW-YORK
FOUNDED IN
MDCCCLXXXV
THE
DUNLAP SOCIETY

BUNKER-HILL

OR

THE DEATH OF GENERAL WARREN

An Historic Tragedy in Five Acts

BY

JOHN BURK

WITH AN INTRODUCTORY ESSAY BY BRANDER MATTHEWS

BURT FRANKLIN, NEW YORK

Published by LENOX HILL Pub. & Dist. Co. (Burt Franklin)
235 East 44th St., New York, N.Y. 10017
Originally Published: 1891
Reprinted: 1970
Printed in the U.S.A.

S.B.N.: 8337-04230
Library of Congress Card Catalog No.: 78-130091
Burt Franklin: Research and Source Works Series 573
Theatre and Drama Series 12

Reprinted from the original edition in the New York Public Library.

INTRODUCTION.

ONE of the most curious chapters in Mr. Laurence Hutton's "Curiosities of the American Stage" is that on "The Revolutionary and War Drama" of these States; and no play which he therein mentions is more curious than Burk's "Bunker-Hill; or the Death of General Warren," an historic tragedy in five acts, first performed in Boston in 1797, a year before Dunlap's "André" was produced. What manner of play "Bunker-Hill" is the reader may see for himself in the following pages. What manner of man its author was it is now difficult to declare with any approach to precision.

John Burk was an Irishman, of the family of the statesman, and so naturally endowed with a love for the Sublime and the Beautiful. He was born apparently within a year or so of the death of General Warren, whose stage-funeral he was to conduct with pomp and florid rhetoric. While a student at Trinity College, Dublin, he was an ardent politician and involved himself in difficulties with the authorities. It is said that he belonged to a secret political society, and that he attempted the rescue of a rebel on his way to execution. He escaped through a bookseller's shop, and while his Irish wolf-dog kept the police at bay he fled, in woman's apparel given him by a Miss Daly.

He escaped to America, as many an Irishman of spirit has done since; and in gratitude to the lady who had aided his flight, he often thereafter signed himself John Daly Burk. Like the late John Boyle O'Reilly, with whose career his has more than one point of resemblance, he settled in Boston and he set up as editor of a newspaper. He had been but a short time in the United States when he published the first number of the *Polar Star and Boston Daily Advertiser*, which bore the date of October 6, 1796. The last number which Mr. Buckingham, the historian of Boston journalism, was able to discover, was dated February 2, 1797; apparently the *Polar Star* remained above the horizon barely six months and then sank forever into the blackness of night.

Perhaps it was this stellar dissolution which led the restless Irishman to leave Boston for New-York. Buckingham tells us that Burk was the editor of a New-York newspaper called the *Time-Piece*, and that he "was arrested on a charge of publishing a libel contrary to the provisions of the sedition law of 1798." How long the new paper told New-Yorkers the time of day I do not know, nor how soon it was that Burk left New-York as he had left Boston. He pushed on as far south as Virginia and settled in Petersburg. In 1804 he published three volumes of a "History of Virginia." In 1808—on the 11th of April—he was killed in a duel with a Frenchman named Coquebert; as far as I can ascertain from the wandering and conflicting "Materials to Serve for a Brief Memoir of John Daly Burk," which Mr. Charles Campbell issued in Albany, in 1868, the provocation came from Burk, at all times hot-headed and loose-tongued.

Besides the "History of Virginia"—a fourth volume of which, by Skelton Jones and Louis Huc, was issued after his death—Burk seems to have been the author of a "History of the Late War in Ireland, with an Account of the United Irish Association, from the

First Meeting in Belfast, to the Landing of the French at Kilala," an octavo volume published in Philadelphia, in 1799. He wrote also "An Historical Essay on the Character and Antiquity of Irish Songs," published in the *Richmond Enquirer*, in May, 1808.

In the appendix to Dunlap's "History of the American Theater," a list is given of all the plays written in America up to the year when Dunlap published (1833); and in this list Burke is credited with eight dramatic pieces. One is the "Bunker-Hill; or the Death of General Warren" herewith reprinted. The second is a "Joan of Arc" acted at the Park Theater, New-York, in April, 1798. A third is "The Death of General Montgomery in storming the City of Quebec": a tragedy, published in Philadelphia in 1797. A fourth is "Bethlem Gabor, Lord of Transylvania, or the Man-Hating Palatine; an Historical Drama in three acts," published in 1807 at Petersburg, and acted both on the regular stage and by the author and fellow-amateurs. Of the other four plays I know nothing but their names, "Female Patriotism," "Fortunes of Nigel," "Innkeeper of Abbeville," and "Which do you like best, the Poor Man or the Lord?" I have a copy of "Bethlem Gabor," and it is a most amusing production, more amusing even than "Bunker-Hill"; but I confess to an intense desire to get hold of a copy of "Which do you like best, the Poor Man or the Lord?" The title promises entertainment unequaled even by Burk's other plays.

As to the first performance of "Bunker-Hill" I cannot do better than quote the account given by Mr. Clapp in his invaluable "Records of the Boston Stage":—

"The Haymarket brought out a piece called 'Bunker Hill, or, the Death of General Warren,' written by John Burk, the editor. As the same piece, or an adaptation, is performed occasionally, we give the first bill:

In Honor of the
CENTENNIAL CELEBRATION OF THE BATTLE OF BUNKER HILL.
HAYMARKET THEATRE.
(Never performed.)

THIS EVENING, FEBRUARY 17, will be presented a tragedy entitled

THE BATTLE OF BUNKER HILL, OR THE DEATH OF GENERAL WARREN.
Written by Mr. Burk.

Gen. Warren, Commander at Bunker Hill.......... Mr. Barrett
Col. Prescott } Major-generals in the American Army. .... Mr. S. Powell
Col. Putnam } .... Mr. Hughes
Gov. Gage. .... Mr. Marriott | Gen. Howe...... Mr. Dickson
Lord Percy... Mr. Williamson | Col. Harman .... Mr. Fawcett
American Grenadier .... Mr. Wilson
Officers, soldiers and attendants, by the rest of the company. And
Col. Abercrombie, in love with and beloved by Elvira, an American lady, captive in Boston........... Mr. Taylor
Anna, attendant on Elvira .... Mrs. Hughes
and Elvira, American captive..................... Mrs. Barrett

To conclude with a grand procession in honor of Warren, whose dead body is borne across the stage on a bier — the American Army moving slowly to the sound of solemn martial music — young women dressed in white, holding flowers in their hands, each with one hand on the bier, will accompany the procession. At proper intervals, flags will display Republican emblems and popular devices.

Principal Mourner and Singer................ Miss Broadhurst
who will introduce an original patriotic elegy, to the much-admired tune of Roslin Castle, over the bier of Warren.
Second Singer and Mourner .... Mme. Pick
Third ..... Miss Eliz. Westray | Fifth .... Miss Westray
Fourth .... Miss Gowen | Sixth..... Miss Eleo. Westray
The Prologue to be spoken by.................. Mr. Powell
Scenery incidental to the piece painted by.......... Mr. Audain

American music only will be played between the acts.

To which will be added the favorite musical entertainment called THE PADLOCK.

Vivat Respublica.

"At that time it was well received, the British being well peppered, and the 'stars and stripes' floating triumphant. It was local in character, and the scene was laid in Charlestown and Boston. Mr. Dickson personated *General Howe*, and how acceptably may be judged from the fact that the author made $2000 by the play. . . .

"We have heard one or two anecdotes of this piece which are too good to be lost. The company attached to the Boston Theatre, during the summer vacation, generally visited some of the provincial towns. On one occasion, while at Portland, Mr. Dickson appeared in the play as *Colonel Abercrombie*, who, wishing to marry an American lady, is told that he must desert the cause of the British and embrace the American side. In this dilemma he soliloquizes, exclaiming: 'Heavens! that madness should so bereave a man of his senses as to doubt which of the two to choose — love or honor.' 'It generally does, Mr. Dickson,' exclaimed a voice in the pit, which called forth shouts of laughter. The person who had thus given his opinion was Mr. George, for many years an editor in that city — an unfortunate cripple, who was especially licensed, by public consent, to say what he thought, without regard to time or place. On another occasion an actor came out to announce the play of the following evening. 'Ladies and gentlemen,' said he, 'we thank you for your attendance this evening, and to-morrow night we shall have the honor of presenting you the much admired play of ——;' here the actor's memory proved treacherous — he bungled, and was at a loss what to say, when little George came to his rescue, by exclaiming: 'It is no consequence for you to mention it—the bills are sticking up in the lobby.' The play of 'Bunker Hill' was performed in New York. President Adams, being in the city, was invited to attend, and at the conclusion of the piece he was conducted by the managers and leading actors to his carriage with considerable pomp and show. Mr. Barrett, who had performed *General Warren*, ventured to express the hope that the President had been pleased. 'Sir,' replied Mr. Adams, 'my friend General Warren was a scholar and a gentleman, but your author has made him a bully and a blackguard.' Mr. Adams's critique was at once concise and correct."

Dunlap, in his "History," quotes a letter from the manager of the Federal Street Theater, in Boston, the opposition house declaring that "two theatres cannot be supported—an additional public could not be created with an additional theatre. Could the *joint* receipts of *both houses* be fairly averaged, I will venture to assert they would not exceed *five hundred and fifty* dollars, while we are expending upwards of *twelve hundred* nightly, to take—'a plague upon both the houses'—the deficiency must fall somewhere. However, we *pay* punctually—it is in proof that our opponents *do not*. They have brought out a new piece called *Bunker's Hill*, a tragedy, the most execrable of the Grub Street kind—but, from its locality in title, the burning of Charlestown and *peppering* the *British* (which are superadded to the tragedy in pantomime), to the utter disgrace of Boston theatricals, has brought them *full houses*."

Dunlap also gives the letter which the author wrote to the manager of the New-York Theater, and this is too characteristic not to be quoted here in full: —

"To J. Hodgkinson, Esq.

"*Dear Sir:* From a wish that you should be possessed of my plays as early as possible, I have preferred sending on the original copy rather than wait to have a fair one transcribed — where it was incomplete I have written and made it good, interspersing occasionally such remarks as, from seeing the effect in representation, appeared to me serviceable in getting it up. It was played seven nights successively, and on the last night was received with the same enthusiasm as on the first — it revived old scenes, and united all parts of the house. Mr. Powell intends it for a stock play, and it will be represented on all festivals — such as 4th July, 17th June, etc. It will be played here in a few nights again, immediately after 'Columbus.' The lines marked by inverted commas are those spoken. The hill is raised gradually by boards extended from the stage to a bench. Three men should walk abreast on it, and the side where the English march up should, for the most part, be turned towards the wings; on our hill there was room for eighteen or twenty men, and they were concealed by a board painted mud-color, and having two cannon painted on it — which board was three feet and a half high. The English marched in two divisions from one extremity of the stage, where they ranged after coming from the wings; when they come to the foot of the hill, the Americans fire — the English fire — six or seven of your men should be taught to fall — the fire should be frequent for some minutes. The English retire to the front of the stage — second time of English advance from the wing near the hill — firing commences — they are again beaten back — windows on the stage should be open to let the smoke out. Again the English make the attack and mount the hill. After a brisk fire the Americans leave works and meet them. Here is room for effect, if the scuffle be nicely managed. Sometimes the English fall back, sometimes the Americans — two or three Englishmen rolling down the hill. A square piece about nine feet high and five wide, having some houses and a meeting-house painted on fire, with flame and smoke issuing from it, should be raised two feet distance from the horizon scene at the back of your stage; the windows and doors cut out for transparencies — in a word, it should have the appearance of a town on fire. We had painted smoke suspended — it is raised at the back wing, and is intended to represent Charlestown, and is on a line with the hill; and where it is lowest, the fire should be played skillfully behind this burning town, and the smoke to evaporate. When the curtain rises in the fifth, the appearance of the whole is good — Charlestown on fire, the breastwork of wood, the Americans appearing over the works and the muzzles of their guns, the English and the American music, the attack of the hill, the falling of the English troops, Warren's half descending the hill, and animating the American's, the smoke and confusion, altogether produce an effect scarce credible. We had a scene of State street—if you had one it would not be amiss—we used it instead of the scene of Boston Neck—it appears to me you need not be particular, but the hill and Charlestown on fire. We had English uniforms for men and officers. You can procure the coats of some company in New York which dresses in red. Small cannon should be fired during the battle, which continued with us from twelve to fifteen minutes. I am thus prolix that you may find less difficulty in getting it up—it is not expensive, and will always be a valuable stock piece. I should not wonder if every person in New York and some miles around it should go to see it represented. There will no doubt be some who will call in question your prudence in getting up this piece, as being not in favor of England. Those are blockheads, and know not the public opinion in America. Boston is as much divided as New York—party was forgotten in the representation of it. Others there are who will endeavor to prejudice you against its merit—of them I shall say nothing. You have the play and can judge for yourself—my reason for mentioning the latter description of men is, that a man from Boston, who pretends to criticise without knowing how to *spell*, has been industrious in depreciating the value of my piece in Boston, and I conceived it not improbable that he would act in the same manner in New York. When he found it had succeeded, he ascribed its success alone to its locality. This man took a letter to you from Mr. Barrett. I send you the prologue and elegy.

"After consulting Mr. Barrett, who was delicate in advising, lest he should be thought partial to one interest or the other, I have concluded to charge you one hundred guineas for the copy, seventy of which I request you will send to Mr. Barrett immediately on receipt of the piece, the remaining thirty on the fourth night of representation. Mr. Barrett thinks it will run ten nights in succession at New York. I think not of printing it for one year; when I do I shall dedicate it to the President. Mr. Bates has sent on to me for a copy. I am in treaty with Mr. Wignell. The terms shall not be lower than with you. I shall send you on from time to time such pantomimes and entertainments as I shall arrange, on reasonable terms. I have three at present, which I shall send on when you please, as cheap as you can get a pirated copy of a farce. My new tragedy, entitled 'Joan of Arc, or the Maid of Orleans,' is ready for representation. Excuse this wretched scrawl — it has been written too hastily.

"JOHN BURK.

"We had our hill on the left side of the stage — the painting of Charlestown on fire should not be seen till the fifth act. If there is anything you would wish to be informed on further, by directing a line to me you shall receive the speediest answer. As I look on this only as the *basis* of a future negotiation, I shall not be averse to abating something of my demand, if you think it high, though I am tolerably certain you will clear four thousand dollars in its run only."

The New-York manager sent back the manuscript at once, only to receive it again with a letter from the author offering it on the terms usually given for new plays. It was produced at the John Street Theater in New-York on the 8th of September, 1797, with the following cast:

Gen. Warren	Mr. Barrett
Lord Percy	Mr. Whitelock
Abercrombie	Mr. Williamson
Gen. Prescott	Mr. Downie
Gen. Putnam	Mr. Hughes
Sir Wm. Howe	Mr. Sully
Harman	Mr. Clough
American Grenadier	Mr. Crosby
Elvira	Mrs. Barrett
Anna	Mrs. Hughes

Mr. Ireland informs us (" Records of the New-York Stage," i. 152) that " the success of the play, though not at all equal to the author's expectations, was more than commensurate with its deserts." When President Adams attended the theater, one night in October, " Bunker-Hill " was the chief play of the evening. It was revived at the Park Theater, New-York, in June, 1799.

And outside of Boston and New-York, Burk's tragedy was also received with popular approval. From the following paragraph of Mr. Charles Blake's "Historical Account of the Providence Stage," published in 1868, it would seem that "Bunker-Hill" retained its attraction through the first half of this century:

"In November for Mr. Barrett's benefit was produced, for the first time in Providence, the new tragedy of 'Bunker Hill,' a miserable compound of fustian, which has proved very remunerative to the theatrical treasury in Boston. It was well received here, and the company then left town, to produce it in Newport. Miserable as the play was it survived many dramas superior to it in every respect, and is now sometimes brought out on the fourth of July in New England cities for the benefit of visitors from the rural districts. It has an history of its own. It was written when politicians indulged in party feelings with a virulence now unknown, and which was wont to seek expression at the theater. The design of the author was to gratify the animosities of the anti-federalist portion of the public, and it was originally produced in Boston at a theatre raised by democratic subscriptions for the purpose of establishing a democratic drama."

I know two editions of Burk's masterpiece, both now in my possession. One has served for this reprint, and its title-page will be found a few pages further on. The other is a smaller pamphlet of the size well known to all collectors of books about the stage as that of Longworth's editions. Its title-page is reproduced on the following page.

BUNKER-HILL;

OR, THE

DEATH OF GENERAL WARREN:

AN HISTORIC TRAGEDY,

IN FIVE ACTS.

BY JOHN BURK,
Late of Trinity-College, Dublin.

AS PERFORMED AT THE THEATRES IN AMERICA, FOR FOURTEEN NIGHTS, WITH UNBOUNDED APPLAUSE.

NEW-YORK:

PUBLISHED BY D. LONGWORTH,
At the Dramatic Repository,
Shakspeare-Gallery.

July—1817.

Of the literary merits of "Bunker-Hill" I do not dare trust myself to speak. I am conscious that they transcend my powers of analysis. The tragedy seems to me as interesting not only in itself — whatever the nature of the interest — but also as throwing light on predilections of our ancestors, the Bostonians and New-Yorkers of the last years of the last century. And perhaps — if any play which pleases us to-day survive till the second centenary of this republic — our descendants of the next century will consider it curiously, and patronizingly speculate on the characteristics of the playgoer of 1891.

BRANDER MATTHEWS.

THE PLAYERS, December, 1891.

Reprinted from The Century Magazine, by permission.

THE PARK THEATER, 1831.

BUNKER-HILL;

OR THE

DEATH OF GENERAL WARREN:

AN

HISTORIC TRAGEDY.

IN

FIVE ACTS.

BY JOHN BURK,
LATE OF TRINITY COLLEGE, DUBLIN.

AS PLAYED AT THE THEATRES IN AMERICA, FOR FOURTEEN NIGHTS, WITH UNBOUNDED APPLAUSE.

NEW-YORK: PRINTED BY T. GREENLEAF.

M,DCC,XCVII.

Dedication.

Sir,

Tho' averse from pride as well as principle, to personal dedications, in which an Author, in search of a patron, generally sacrifices his love of truth and independence; and though in obedience to this opinion, I have permitted many Compositions to go undedicated, and unpatronized on the world; for once, to indulge a sentiment of private gratitude and esteem, I depart from my system, and present to you my Tragedy of Bunker Hill. I shall find few difficulties in justifying to myself this individualism, when I reflect with what courage and patriotism you stepped forward to fight the battles of your country, to one of which I am indebted for the subject of my drama: But I fear I shall not so easily justify myself to you and the public, from the imputation of presumption in intruding on the importance of your time, and the lustre of your talents and erudition, a trifle so every way unworthy of you. To the later I only can say, it is my best offering; and had it been better, it should have the same direction. With earnest wishes for the success of the piece and its patron, praying a length of years and encrease of honors for both,

I am,

With esteem and respect,

Your's.

J. BURK.

Aaron Burr, Esq.

PROLOGUE — BY THE AUTHOR.

WHEN o'er Columbia's fields in fearful hour,
Glared the red Comet of Britannia's power,
From horrid hair shook flakes of burning wrath,
And war and desolation mark'd its path:
Rous'd by the fury of her ruthless foes,
The angry Genius of Columbia rose:
Then, with a voice more loud, more deep than fate,
Was rent the fabric of Monarchic State,
And instantaneous, soothing as the lyre,
Which wakes the soul and kindles soft desire,
She called the *great Republic* into day,
And to a world, restored its legal sway:
Behold; her patriot band the low lands fills
Like to the torrents of a thousand hills,
Which thund'ring to the plain their waters roll,
Unite, condense, and form a mighty whole;
Columbia's Sons down Alleghany's sides,
Their fiery cohorts pour in rapid tides:
Whilst o'er the glassy surface of the flood,
Light'd by the Sun, a gallant vessel rode;
The Ark which bears the charter of the land,
It sails directed by the Almighty hand:
'Till safe at length from tempest and from flood,
Secure on freedom's Ararat it stood.
Thus did this great, this glorious Empire rise,
Which lifts its patriot honors to the skies;
Spite of the bloody lash, the tyrant's frown,
The shock of armies and a fleet's renown.

A nobler theme than this, to grace the stage,
Where can we find in all th' historic page?
Of Rome's and Cato's fall, the World has rung:
Why not Columbia's rising fame be sung?
If Rome her Brutus and her Cato boast;
Her Washington and Warren, each a host,
Columbia owns; with thousand names beside,
The least of which would swell the Roman pride:
And midst these themes sublime, these subjects grand
Which tempt the poet's fancy in this land,
Where is there one more potent to inspire
Conceptions vast, and wake Parnassian fire,
Than when on Bunker's top a glorious band
Pour'd out their sacred blood to save the land?
And ere they fell, such fierce destruction hurl'd,
As when Volcanoes burn and tear the world.
Such is our Bard's excuse that he this night
Renews the horrors of fam'd Bunker's fight,
And, bending suppliant at your awful shrine,
His Child to your protection doth consign:
Assur'd of Justice, he has dar'd to trace,
Columbia's Glories to *Columbia's* race.

DRAMATIS PERSONÆ.

General Warren,	Mr. Barrett.
Lord Percy,	Mr. Williamson.
General Prescott,	Mr. S. Powell.
General Putnam,	Mr. Hughes.
Governor Gage,	Mr. Marriot.
Sir William Howe,	Mr. Dickinson.
American Grenadier,	Mr. Wilson.
Abercrombie,	Mr. Taylor.

American Officers, Soldiers, and Attendants.

Anna,	Mrs. Hughes.
Elvira,	Mrs. Barrett.

Bunker-Hill.

ACT I.

SCENE. *A View of* BOSTON *from Roxbury Neck. A Party of English fly across the Stage as if pursued.* LORD PERCY *faint, and leaning on his Sword is addressed by* GOVERNOR GAGE.

HOW's this my Lord!
What means this shameful rout among the troops!
But lately from these gates they issued
In all the proud array of glorious war,
Looking as if they were invincible:
Now pale dismay affrights them; they appear
Worn down by heat, and want of sustenance;
Afflicted, sprightless, desiring rest
More than renown! Speak, I guess the truth!
But yet it cannot be, that senseless rebels,
Brave only in a mob when pillage calls
And loud sedition gathers them together,
Should cope with discipline, or knee to knee
The sun burnt veteran combat.

LORD PERCY.

Your Excellency shall be satisfied
In each particular of this toilsome day,
So fatal to our Warriors; but first,
Let the drums beat to arms, man all the works,
For if I do mistake not, ere the night
Shall o'er the town her dusky mantle draw,
A furious foe will thunder at our posts.

GOV. GAGE.

It shall be done: but yet it cannot be,
That all at once they will assume such boldness,
And shew Rebellion's face without a mask:
However, they shall find here such reception,
As will, if they approach, their ardor damp,
And make them think their former chains a blessing
When measured with the heavier punishment
Of bayonet and cannon.
Harman, ho: [*calls to one of his aids*]
Let all the guards be doubled; [*Enter* HARMAN]
Look to your guns and see them charg'd with grape,
And more than usual vigilance command
To all the sentinels [*Officer bows and exit*].
[*Turns to* LORD PERCY]
Now my Lord,
I wait impatiently for thy account
Of this strange business.

LORD PERCY.

According to your Excellency's orders,
With the detachment under my command,

I posted on to Lexington; with a view
To succour Smith, or take what other course
Requir'd by circumstances; judge my surprize,
When I beheld Smith's party in full rout,
With thousands and ten thousands at his heels,
All order fled, confusion through the ranks
Stalking with death and terror in his train:
In haste I form'd my forces to repel
The numbers which assail'd him: for a while
My cannon kept the foe at distance,
But soon their numbers so encreased, and fury
Beyond all calculation; and beside
Their trim and movements seem'd so soldier like,
That fearing for the safety of the troops
Committed to my charge, I thought it best
With all convenient speed to hasten back,
Lest these rebellious townsmen should attack
The quarters in our absence, and cut off
All intercourse between the troops and Boston:
But tho' the wisest measures were adopted
For this retreat, they hung upon our rear,
Rushing on with fury next to madness;
Till every inch of ground was bought with blood.

GOV. GAGE.

I thought two thousand British troops might march
Through all America! driving before them,
Like chaff, th' affrighted colonists. How in England
Will sound this news; too distant to observe,
Our names will be the subject of reproach:
For they will ne'er believe a peasant rout,

Unexperienc'd to arms, unus'd to War,
Could stand before a British soldiery,
Unless by some misconduct in their chiefs.
Beside, 'twill have another bad effect:
The spirits of those rebels will be rais'd,
Before too high: like rivers swell'd by rain,
Which spurn the narrow limits of their banks;
Their hearts will swell with arrogance and pride;
Our discipline and order will be slighted;
Our military character contemn'd,
Which oftener gains the battle than the sword:
But did you well observe their countenance;
Did it but seem the flash of short liv'd anger,
Which pushed them on; or the determin'd frown
Which marks the settled purpose of the mind.

LORD PERCY.

Imagine to yourself the Roman legion,
Or Grecian phalanx rang'd in battalia;
The furious aspect of the ancient Gaul,
Or painted Briton our brave ancestor:
Think all their terrors center'd in the foe,
With whom we wrestled: 'twill be near the truth:
Whilst on our march a thousand fierce attacks
Rag'd on our rear; when we fac'd about,
Like the incursive Parthians they were gone:
Again we march'd, again the battle rag'd.

GOV. GAGE.

This business is unlucky;
Our project was to keep the shew of friendship,

And seem as if we would concede, till troops
Arriv'd from England; but this affair
Has disconcerted all our best laid schemes.
Now all America will rise in arms,
And thus a war, which in its infancy
Might have been crush'd with ease, will yet remain
An heritage to our posterity —
Or, leave these rebels masters of this land.

LORD PERCY.

Your Excellency has not yet enquired
What loss our troops sustained at Lexington.

GOV. GAGE.

Ay very true; my mind was so engaged
With doubts and apprehensions I forgot it.
Have you yet muster'd them?

LORD PERCY.

I have my lord:
And I am griev'd to tell you, that one half
Of Colonel Smith's detachment is cut off.

GOV. GAGE.

By heaven this business is alarming!
Now fame will bear the tidings of this loss
Thro' all this continent; exaggerating all,
Destroying ten for every one that dy'd:
And those Americans will so exult,
As when, of old, the Mexicans they bore
The head of a slain Spaniard, through the land;

To shew the people that the foe was mortal:
The weak and timid now will lose their fears
Of our experience and our discipline;
And those who trembled at a soldier's cap
Will henceforth dash defiance in our teeth.

[*Enter an Officer in haste.*]

OFFICER.

May it please your Excellency——

GOV. GAGE.

What tidings do you bear?

OFFICER.

As on the isthmus we patrol'd the lines
To see that all the passes were secur'd,
According to your Excellency's orders,
A cloud of dust approaching to the town
Darken'd the air—instant we sent scouts,
Who, breathless with affright and haste, return'd
With information, that the foe was near
And hither bent their course.

LORD PERCY.

I told your Excellency it would be so.

GOV. GAGE.

This seems to speak the foe in earnest:
But let them come; they spare us the fatigue
Of following them: blow winds from England,

And waft the British navy to these shores:
We then shall pay these Mutineers with interest:
Their Chiefs and Senators shall grace the gibbet,
Whilst on the vulgar herd we'll heap subjection,
'Till that their bones do ache.

Exeunt.

[ABERCROMBIE *comes on as they go off.*]

ABERCROMBIE, *solus.*

Such are the men who sow this world with broils:
Incendiaries, who blow the coals of war,
And civil strife and havoc loose abroad:
Unhappy England! how art thou abus'd?
Alas my Country, I foresee thy fate:
A prey to hungry courtiers, thou wilt fall
Like ancient Rome when she had lost her rights.
A cursed junto, like Prometheus' vulture,
Lives on thy vitals; but more voracious:
'Tis not enough for them to drink thy blood,
But they must turn their carrion stained beaks,
To tear the bowels of these guiltless shores:
Such is the British government, and such,
Must ever be the government of kings:
I know that in the world's opinion,
I shall be deem'd a man of little wisdom
For reasoning thus; what care I for the world?
Love has resign'd my soul,
And stript it of those merciless resolves,
Those sanguinary politics, inspir'd
By regal pride; no more I look on man
As born my enemy, because we live

On different sides of rivers, or of lakes;
I love the race of man in every clime:
Elvira, peerless maid, hath wrought this change;
O might I pass with her, remote from war,
In some sequester'd dale my span of life:
The pageantry of camps should be resigned.
But ah vain wish! like to the galley slave,
Chain'd down by honor, to the cannon's breech,
I have no choice, no agency of will.

[*Enter* ELVIRA *and* ANNA, *she beckons* ANNA.]

Elvira! what busy thoughts have call'd thy gentle limbs,
At such an hour as this, from calm repose?
Scarce has the Nightingale withdrawn his song,
And left the field's dominion to the lark:
'Tis yet but grey ey'd morn, and the air
Keen edg'd with east wind's coldness would offend
A coarser form than thine; how then, sweet maid,
Dost thou in cold's defiance venture here.

ELVIRA.

Oppress'd by care, I pass'd a sleepless night;
Griev'd by the thought of what my parents feel,
Uncertain of my fate, and fill'd with fears
Of the rude elements and ruder war:
Bold fancy conjur'd up a thousand forms,
And frightful images of black despair,
To haunt my slumbers; at length, fatigu'd
With tossing to and fro, I left my chamber,
And hasted here to taste the essenc'd breeze,
Which on the dewy pinions of the morn

Is borne from off the sea; beside I wish'd,
From yonder eminence, to view the hosts
Which gird this city round, if by some chance
The face of friend or kinsman I might see
Amongst the shining squadrons.

ABERCROMBIE.

Lovely Elvira, may I without offence thy promise claim
To tell thy story; oft have I observed
Thy lovely face o'ercast with melancholy;
Oft have I mark'd the sigh escape thy breast,
Seen the tear start in my Elvira's eye;
Hide not thy griefs from me, not thy own soul
Can feel them with more poignance.

ELVIRA.

My friend I know it;
And should but make a poor return, indeed;
Was I to answer thee with cold denial.
My father in the Carolinas lives,
A wealthy man and high in reputation
Acquired in our continental wars,
What time the warlike French their inroads made,
To spoil the borders of your provinces;
Me, his sole daughter, he to England sent,
At earnest wish of his beloved sister,
Who rich and childless begg'd me for her own:
With her, three years I liv'd, 'till cruel death
Depriv'd me of her care; my father then
His brother sent in one of his own ships,
To lead me back again to Carolina:

From him I learnt the tyranny of England,
The near approach of war, and that my father,
Fir'd with the love of freedom, had resolv'd,
To join his country: when we reach'd this coast,
An English cruiser seiz'd upon our bark,
And brought us into Boston; what follow'd then
Thou best can tell, who with a brother's care
Reliev'dst me from the worst of ills, dishonour.

ABERCROMBIE.

Alas! I see the ruin of my hopes
In this short story; I am an English soldier,
Sent here, to rob thy country of its rights:
As such, thy father must reject my suit;
He must detest me as the sworn foe
Of all that he holds dear.

ELVIRA.

Thou know'st him not;
He is a grateful, wise, and generous man.

ABERCROMBIE.

There lie my fears;
Had he been one, amongst the vulgar herd,
Devoid of sense, unprincipled;
Who, like the present race of warlike men,
For wretched hire would fight on any side,
It might be easy to succeed with him;
But as he is, the soldier of his country,
The champion of her rights, he will detest me
For fighting in the cause of despotism.

ELVIRA.

I'll tell him that thou hat'st the present measures,
And mean'st to leave the service.

ABERCROMBIE.

Not for the world:
Much as I love thee, I love honor more;
How would my friends in England feel to hear
That in the teeth of danger I resign'd,
And on the eve of battle left the camp?
They could not, would not comprehend my scruples,
And to ignobler motives may ascribe
What flow'd from justice and conviction.

ELVIRA.

It cannot be dishonor to resign
When murder takes the place of generous war!
When frantic tyrants, arm'd with savage rage,
Direct their baneful march through peaceful fields,
Wasting with fire and sword the peasants' toil!
No Abercrombie, honour calls the soul
From scenes of blood to taste the purer joys
Which spring from social life.

ABERCROMBIE.

Thus will thy father argue, thus declaim;
Thus will he reason on the crimes of kings;
And thus alas will he destroy my hopes:
My soul approves of all, that thou hast said:
And was I sure my conduct would be judg'd
By such as thee, so prudent and so pure,

Long since decision would have crown'd thy wish;
But as it is, when flimsy fashion rules,
And guides the helm where honour should preside,
'Twere madness so to risk my reputation.

ELVIRA.

And canst thou then, to humour paltry fashion,
Go coolly forth to shed thy brother's blood?
How differently did Cato think of honor!
Its semblance he despis'd, but to itself
He clung with all the constancy of Cato.

ABERCROMBIE.

Surely Elvira doth not wish to see
Her friend dishonor'd!

ELVIRA.

Heaven is my witness;
Thy honour is not dearer to thyself.

ABERCROMBIE.

Sweet maid, I crave thy pardon; I know it;
I am unworthy of such matchless worth:
What shall I do? O counsel me Elvira;
Be my good angel and direct my cause.

ELVIRA.

Alas! what can I do that I will not;
But when before,
I counsel'd thee in love's and reason's voice,
And spoke the artless language of the soul,

My suit thou didst reject; O now again
Let me my former admonition urge;
Forsake the hateful standard of oppression;
And with Elvira and her father live,
Bless'd with the gifts of fortune and of love.

ABERCROMBIE.

Dearest Elvira.
How good art thou, and how unworthy I:
This day at three o'clock I'll meet thee here,
For now my hour it is t' relieve the guard,
Which watches on the neck — till then farewell.

ELVIRA.

Farewell.
Let not the gorgeous pomp of laurell'd war
Seduce thy mind from me.

[*Go off at different sides.*]

ACT II.

SCENE — A CHAMBER.

GEN. WARREN *seated at a table, holds a letter in his hand announcing the defeat of the British at Lexington.*

At length the sun of freedom 'gins to rise
Upon the world; a glorious dawn of day,
Breaking in lucid streaks of every hue,
Shedding its incens'd breathing on the mind:
And the deep night, where tyrants sat enthron'd,
Shrouding their horrid forms from the world,
Now passes on, like mists before the sun.
The day is come for which through every age
Sages have sighed; which like a magic spell,
Shall dash down tyrants and their thrones together,
And make their blood-stain'd idols fall before it;
Too long the world has groan'd beneath the yoke
Of frantic despotism; war followed war,
And horrid rage deform'd the works of heaven.
Now a new era rises on the world;
The spirit of old Rome inspires the land;
Fir'd with a glorious ardor, young and old

Fly to the field, determin'd to assert
Those sacred rights, which nature hath design'd
Alike, for all the children of this earth.
And shall I then, inglorious, stay behind,
While my brave countrymen are braving death
To purchase glory; I too am fond of glory,
And such a cause will make ambition, virtue.
But I can do good service otherwise;
By writing, I can help the public cause,
And heal my brethren wounded in the fight.
'Tis cowardice that reasons: *all* is best.
I never heard that Brutus was content,
That he had done just so much, and no more;
No — Liberty will ne'er be woo'd by halves,
But like the jealous female, must have all
The lover's heart or none: but then again —
I am not young, and feel beside, the ties
Of family endearments; what of that?
Was Cato young, or had he no connections,
When thro' Numidia's burning sands he led
His little Senate in pursuit of freedom;
Preferring pain and every ill to bondage?
Was Cincinnatus young, when from the plough,
Call'd by his country's voice, he flew to battle?
The patriot should o'erleap all obstacles
Which stand between him and his darling country;
Not age, not sex, nor scarcely pain itself,
Should be exempt from this important duty,
But ALL before the sacred voice of country,
When to her children she doth cry for succour,
Should fly to her relief, and guard from insult,

The soil, which holds the bones of their forefathers;
This sentiment is heavenly, and doth bind
The wandering Tartar to the little spot,
Where the dead bodies of his tribe are laid:
How then can the remainder of my life,
Be better spent, than in my country's service?
A thousand bright examples point the way,
Trodden by heroes: shall I then keep back,
When such a glorious harvest may be won?
No — from this hour, my resolution's fixt:
Here in the face of heaven, I devote [*kneels.*]
Myself, my services, my life to Freedcm; [*rises.*]
And I can think of nothing but of souls,
Who in contempt of death their country sav'd;
Of Curtius, of Scœvola and of Brutus,
Of Cato, Cassius, Decii and Camilli;
And if to these, sweet heaven, I could add
The name of Warren, and hand them together
Down in succession to posterity,
By heaven I'd gladly meet their hardest fate
And think my life well lost to merit it.

[*A knock at the door.*]

Come in —

[*Enter a Servant.*]

A stranger waits below to see you sir,
On business, as he says, of consequence.

WARREN.

Shew him up stairs.

[*Servant bows and exit and shortly after enters with an officer.*]

OFFICER.

Just from the camp arriv'd, I bear to thee
A message from the soldiers and their chiefs:
With one consent, they have deputed me
To call thee to command.

WARREN.

Yes, I will go;
And share with them the hardships of the war:
Whether as private, or as leader rang'd;
My post is honor and my country's good.
But was all quiet; did the troops retain
The spirit which prevail'd at Lexington?

OFFICER.

The army grows in spirit every hour:
Scarce can the chiefs restrain their burning ardor;
So strong is their resentment of their wrongs,
That loudly they demand to be led out,
Promising if this be done, they will expell
The British troops from Boston.

WARREN.

Supreme disposer of events! I thank thee:
Now Britain do thy worst, we fear thee not:
Now let thy sultan issue his vain threats,
His windy proclamations to these shores;
They will not scare a baby; knit by love,
Columbia's gallant sons will scorn his rage;
Whilst o'er the ruins of his lawless power,
That pride of human policy, shall rise
A Pure Republic; whose glory shall eclipse

The Roman and the Grecian commonwealths
Much as the sun outshines the dimmed star.
Then Revolutions "*will be so in use*,"
That kings, when they behold the morning break,
Will bless their stars for living one day more.
But while we speak, the battle may be won,
And we have lost our portion of the glory:
Tell the army, my sense of the high favor
Confer'd by them, calls forth my gratitude,
And never, till the mighty debt be paid
To them, and to my country, will I know
Rest or repose; that if no way be found,
But death, to prove my title to their favor,
Why then I die! and swell the glorious list
Of Patriots, who have died for suffering virtue.

OFFICER.

These sentiments are noble;
Worthy the glorious cause which we maintain;
I shall repeat them faithfully, and now
I take my leave, hoping your success
And safe return when the fight is done.

WARREN.

Farewell: and I shall follow close behind thee;
But ere this hand shall grasp the vengeful steel
For one short hour I must put off the soldier,
And on the necks of my bewailing kindred,
Falter a sad farewell; 'tis nature's call:
I feel the father's, and the brother's fears:
Yes, I shall weep 'till the stern frown of war
Is drown'd in tears.

SCENE II.

GENERALS PUTNAM, PRESCOTT.

PRESCOTT.

Well Putnam;
What think you of our troops' appearance?

PUTNAM.

It doth outrun my warmest expectations:
Thro' the whole line I rode along to Mystick,
And not one coward face could I observe;
One soul appear'd to animate them all;
They look'd at once like Patriots and like brothers.

PRESCOTT.

Such were my observations;
Is it yet known if Warren joins the army?

PUTNAM.

This day he is expected at the camp.

PRESCOTT.

I'm glad on it;
Our circumstances call for men of talent,
Whose genius may direct us in the ways
Of untry'd war; but is it not a question,
If he be not more wanted in the cab'net?
His choice alone this question must decide.

PUTNAM.

Then he hath made his choice; and that is war.
His active soul disdains to court repose,
To lie down in the lap of ease and pleasure,
When foreign usurpation frights the land.

PRESCOTT.

So Cato, the great Roman, us'd to act:
When freedom wak'd him from the sleep of peace,
Over his senatorial robe, he threw
The mail of Mars; and stalk'd along to battle,
Terrible to view, as when he fill'd the senate,
And rail'd and thunder'd at the nation's vices.

PUTNAM.

Methinks he does resemble that great Roman:
Exalted by his virtues to the place
Of President of our provincial congress;
It seem'd a'tho' fortune had no more to give,
To raise him higher; yet is he not content,
But must have share in every kind of glory.
[*a shout.*]
What shout is that I hear, perhaps he's come,
And thus it is the Soldiers welcome him.

PRESCOTT.

Most surely it is he:
And yonder comes the great, the honest man,
Bending this way; behold what dignity!

I will suppose that heaven hath sent him here,
To light us in the twilight of the war.

[*Enter* WARREN.]

Welcome, good sir;
It joys me to behold you here amongst us.

PUTNAM.

And me.

WARREN.

I thank you my brave countrymen,
My brothers and companions of the war:
This single day has made me full amends
For all the tedious hours of painful life,
Which I have dragg'd along this wretched land:
I've seen this day, what once not e'en my zeal
Did dare to hope; my country a vast camp,
Glowing with ardor and enthusiasm:
'Tis good; most good: let me but live to see
The English power in these states dissolv'd
I've liv'd then long enough.

PRESCOTT.

That day is not far distant I expect.

PUTNAM.

With such a cause as ours 'twere wrong to doubt.

WARREN.

I have no doubts;
While in our host appear such names as Mercer,

As Prescott, Thomas, Ward, and Washington,
Himself a host; Gates, Hancock and Adams,
Wooster and Putnam, Franklin and Montgomery,
And thousand other names of high repute,
Which forward press to save the sinking state:
Let us leave doubt and terror to our foes:
It better doth become us to salute
Our revolution's dawn, with choral hymns
And songs of gratulation.

PRESCOTT.

There is a name, which in thy list of patriots
Thou hast not mention'd; tho' of equal value
With all the rest.

WARREN.

Many there are, thank heaven, leagued with us,
Whose virtues merit an eulogium:
But none in my opinion
Deserve such high pre-eminence of praise.

PRESCOTT.

Had any but thyself, made out the list
The name of Warren had stood foremost on it.

WARREN.

It might be so, if partial friendship spake:
But yours, and yours and mine and all our stations
Are undetermin'd yet; this war will fix them,
And candid history fearless will decide,

Who best has serv'd his country; then my friends
Let all of us so act that 'twill perplex
Posterity to name the worthiest man:
So that at length, unable to decide,
It leaves the affair in doubt.

PUTNAM.

With what a noble modesty he waives
The praise, which only truth has drawn from us.

[*aside.*]

The counsel sir is good:
But have we yet a plan of operations
Whereon to act;
The English chief but waits a reinforcement,
Which may with every favoring gale arrive
To take the field; methinks this is the time
To strike a blow, while the king's troops are weak
And ours are hot in blood since Lexington.

WARREN.

Thou'rt right my friend;
The foe should have no time to gather strength,
We must alarm him by some rapid movement,
Seize some important post, threaten the town,
Burn the ships, and keep on the alert
To guard against his sallies; this will make
Boston of small advantage; and force him
To quit his holds, and meet us in the field
Or fly back in his ships to Britain.

PUTNAM.

The sufferings of this town afflict my soul:
Fame says that Gage discharges his command
With savage fury; loading the inhabitants
With taunts and injuries: e'en the house of prayer
Is now become a stable; and their horses
When smoaking from the carnage they retire
Their hoofs red with freedom's dearest blood,
Are litter'd there, and by their echoed neighs
Supply the place of worship:

WARREN.

Let him rage on;
Let him exhaust his fury to invent
New modes of torture, for the brave and free;
His hour of fell dominion soon expires,
And execrations then will follow him:
While Boston, glorious town, shall long survive
The fall of monarchies, the sack of states:
And live with Rome and Athens in the page
Of History; great parent of our rights!
How largely hast thou sacrific'd to freedom,
How greatly, hast thou dar'd the tyrant's rage,
How gloriously withstood seduction,
How patiently supported stern misfortune;
By heaven I would not change my station
As citizen of these illustrious states,
To sway the British sceptre.

PRESCOTT.

It is a glorious town.

PUTNAM.

Can nothing be devised for its relief.

WARREN.

Yes, thanks to heaven, this moment I conceive
A plan, which shall afford the wish'd relief:
The post of Bunker Hill commands the town,
The isthmus, with a spacious range beside
Of sea and ships; this will we take by night,
And fortify with all convenient speed
So that our cannon by the morning's dawn,
May play upon the foe.

PUTNAM.

The project is most excellent,
And suits exactly with our circumstances.

PRESCOTT.

One thing alone is wanting to ensure
Success to it:

WARREN.

What is that?

PRESCOTT.

That General Warren should command the troops
Sent on this service.

WARREN.

If that be it, there is no want at all:
Warren will ne'er refuse the post of danger:

8

We have no time to lose, let us propose
The matter in full council; so that night
May hide our motions from the wily foe:
Beside the choicest spirits we must choose
From all the troops; souls, who look down on death
And value freedom more than life itself.

END OF THE SECOND ACT.

ACT III. SCENE I.

ABERCROMBIE, *solus.*

Unhappy Abercrombie!
Dost thou still hold this passion in thy breast?
I am the veriest slave of empty honor,
And yet the truest votary of love:
Heavens can it be, that madness should bereave
A man so of his senses, as to doubt
Which of the two to choose:
This moment, both shall come to settlement;
And I will strike the balance: first for love.
I love Elvira, loveliest of her sex;
And she, sweet maid, above the little arts
Of her light sex; has own'd a mutual flame;
And tries to win me by a thousand arts
Of sweet endearment, to retire with her,
And leave the noisy paths of guilty life.
O extacy! this savors of a tale,
Of lovers, living in the golden age,
Walking o'er flowery fields of fairy joy,
And arm in arm, beguiling lazy time,
By soft caresses:
Next honor comes, and lays before my view,
My great forefathers, who acquir'd great names,
For fighting for their country; and who seem

To frown on me, for tarnishing their fame,
A censuring world putting their soil'd fingers:
On my fair name, and coupling it with coward;
It is too much, there's madness in the thought:
Yes, tyrant fashion! thou shalt be obey'd,
Thou shall be glutted with my life's dear blood.
  But yonder comes the lovely maid herself,
The source of all my hopes, and all my fears;
I must not trust my weak resolves with her,
One look and honor dies.

[*is retiring.*]

ELVIRA.

Stop Abercrombie!
Am I then grown so odious in thy sight,
That thou wilt fly me.

ABERCROMBIE.

Dearest Elvira,
Do not afflict my soul with such reproaches;
By heaven, the light's not dearer to these eyes,
Than is to me thy presence; that alone
Is sunshine to me; that, when I shall lose,
All will be black as night; this world a vault,
Where pleasure lies entomb'd:
Alas I breathe, I live but in thy sight;
But I was willing to conceal my griefs,
Not wound thy tender heart.

ELVIRA.

My dearest friend;
How long wilt thou indulge this gloom of mind;
My father's on his way from Carolina;

So speaks this letter, and will soon arrive:
To thee in liveliest terms, he describes
His gratitude; he calls thee his protector,
Defender of the honor of his house,
And longs t'embrace thee, and to call thee friend.

ABERCROMBIE.

I must not see him.

ELVIRA.

Not see him! you surprize me.

ABERCROMBIE.

The scales, which hold my honor and my love,
Are nicely balanc'd; neither side inclines,
But if thy father's powerful reasoning
Be put 'gainst honor, in the scale with love;
I fear 'twill break the balance.

ELVIRA.

Thou mean'st false honor.

ABERCROMBIE.

I mean the tie, which binds me to my oath;
Know'st thou not, Elvira, I have sworn
Allegiance to the king?

ELVIRA.

My friend I know it;
But the first oath, a solemn binding one,
Enjoin'd by heaven itself; was due from thee,
To nature and thy country; that, my friend,

No after stipulation can expunge;
Surely, if Britain's king commanded thee
To drag thy aged parents from their house,
And murder them, thou art not bound t'obey him.

ABERCROMBIE.

Most certainly I should be disobedient
To such commands!

ELVIRA.

No more, art thou oblig'd to hear his voice,
If drunk with frantic wrath, he order thee
To bear the sword and torch of civil war,
Against thy peacefull, unoffending countrymen.

ABERCROMBIE.

I cannot, must not reason:
Persuasion lurks in every word of thine:
Reject me, hate, despise me, cast me off,
Nor let the sunshine of thy patriot virtues
Be darken'd by uniting with a slave.

ELVIRA.

Hold, my friend;
Thou shalt not so calumniate thyself.
Immortal Brutus scorn'd not fetters more!
But oh! if e'er thy soul did virtue know,
If e'er true honor did obtain from thee
A hearing on thy breast; pluck from thine eye,
The allusive beam, which so discolors objects,
That 'twixt true honor and its opposite
Thou fairly may'st distinguish.

ABERCROMBIE.

Angelic goodness ! soul of innocence,
Pure as the sacred fire, which us'd to burn
In Vesta's temple ; tell we what to do,
That by the execution of thy counsel,
I may deserve thy love.

ELVIRA.

Forsake the hateful standard of oppression !
Elvira then will mourn her lack of virtues,
And pray for more, to make her worthy of thee.

ABERCROMBIE.

Of all things, thou hast mention'd what alone
I must not do :
Bid me ascend grim Niagara's top,
And on its torrent sail the horrid steep,
Stunn'd by the thunder of its falling flood ;
It shall be done : command me to describe
A nautic circle round the various globe ;
As Cook of deathless fame and Anson did,
All, all but honor will I yield to thee.

ELVIRA.

Do I now hear thy final resolution ?

ABERCROMBIE.

Yes, much as the sacrifice costs me I resign thee ;
How dearly thou art lov'd, witness those tears,
Those agonizing drops which wring the soul ;

And here, great heaven! bear witness to my vow;
If to those wretched arms I e'er admit
One of the race of woman, save Elvira,
May barrenness, and care, and want attend
The monstrous union.

[ELVIRA *kneels.*]

And I, here in the presence of the sun,
Do also vow; be witness for me Heaven:
And mark the breach of it by all your vengeance.
If e'er Elvira doth her hand bestow
On any man but thee, may angry heaven,
Even in the bridal hour, its wrath inflict,
And take away her reason.— Farewell, for——ever.

[*Is going.*]

ABERCROMBIE.

Ah, cruel maid! Why dost thou say forever?
The word *farewell*, without it, is enough
To tear my heart; one kiss — one sad embrace —
And then we part.

ELVIRA.

O! cruel fate.
Why did we meet, or why now having met?
Is heaven averse, and frowns upon our love?
O Abercrombie leave this wicked war;
Blest in each other we can bear the taunts,
The idle censures of a worthless world.

ABERCROMBIE.

O thou bewitching goodness, how thou temptest me,
To lay my captive honor at thy feet;

But I must break from thee, I must not stay.
England and honor, every thing forbid it:
Farewell sweet maid, farewell, I fear, forever.

[*Exit.*]

[ELVIRA, *sola.*]

Ha! then he's gone, and gone, mayhap, forever;
And yet I speak, and think, and hold my reason!
Rare flintiness of heart! perhaps this day
He may be sent to battle; this very hour,
E'en while I speak, the order may have come,
And he, O wayward fortune! may have march'd,
And may have died: Why did I not detain him;
Why on my knees did I not pray to him
To stay with me; mayhap I had prevailed;
Won by my tears and sighs, his tender soul
Had been subdued, and we had both been happy.

[*Pauses.*]

But ah Elvira! hast thou not a father,
Whose patriot soul impels him to the fight;
And fear'st thou not for him? lest in the shock,
Pierc'd by a thousand wounds his body lie:
Lest wash'd in blood his hoar locks trail the dust.
Unnatural child — O cruel Pelican —
Is the soft call of nature silenc'd in thee?
Or does the furious spirit of a pard
Thy soul inhabit? 'tis cursed treason:
When like the torrents of a thousand hills,
Glittering in steel, my country moves to battle,
Bearing on its cheek, the flush of independence,
For me to mourn the soldier of a king:
But then how brave, how good the royalist is,

How soft, how pure, how tender, and beside
The saviour of my honour; hateful war—
Thou reeking monster, dear to kings alone,
Thou red destroyer—what a host of ills
Doth follow in thy train. Falls her brave lover,
Or, her patriot sire. Elvira will not live.
[*Exit.*]

AMERICAN CAMP.

Enter WARREN, *at one wing, at the other* HARMAN, *a British officer, preceded by a trumpet and flag of truce.*

GEN. WARREN.

You say you wish to speak with Gen. Warren.

HARMAN.

With that intent, have I been here dispatch'd
By Gen. Gage; who values your endowments,
And thinks too highly of you, not to grieve,
To see you an accomplice in rebellion,
In cursed treason, 'gainst your sovereign:
He has commission'd me, to tell you
That in respect of your unspotted fame,
Your life, and matchless qualities, he sends
Remission of all past offences;
With this condition, that you come to Boston,
And leave the rebel camp.

GEN. WARREN.

Take back this answer to your master:
Tell him the *rebel* Warren, thinks too low
Of his endowments, both of head and heart;

Not to despise his pity and his powers;
How comes he by the right to pardon me,
Insolent man — if heaven hath wrought a change
In his black heart; and soften'd it to pity,
He has the amplest field to shew his mercy;
Boston, town of heroes, calls on him
To sheath the sword, which frights her guiltless sons,
To muzzle up the fury of his slaves,
His abject, murderous, mercenary slaves,
Which shed the townsmen's blood.

HARMAN.

I must not surely take this answer back;
At least his goodness calls for better language.

WARREN.

Goodness! weak man! you know not what you say;
Is 't goodness to seduce the soldier's worth,
To rob of that loftiness of soul,
That pride, which makes him spurn dishonor from him;
To make him a vile traitor, a base slave:
Is this what now in England is call'd goodness?
Rather sweet heaven! than be that abject thing
Your bashaw's goodness wishes me to be,
I'd sink into the meanest drudge at once,
And eat the scanty pittance of hard labour.

HARMAN.

Surely — there's no dishonor in obedience,
No crime in taking you from foul rebellion;

WARREN.

'Tis thou, good sir, who takest this matter wrong;
When nations lose their rights, words of best sense
Are tortur'd to mean what the rulers please;
And the infection has laid hold on you.
Instance *obedience*, which in earliest sense,
Design'd submission to the wisest laws,
Is made to mean a base, unmanly, fawning,
An abject acquiescence under wrongs;
And thus *rebellion*, which of old was us'd
To mark the conduct of a *Catiline*,
Is made to represent the glorious act
Of a *whole people*, bursting from their chains.

HARMAN.

Our English laws are fam'd thro'out the world
For their impartial justice and their mildness,
'Tis therefore rank rebellion, to resist them.

WARREN.

What are your boasted English laws to us,
Or any laws, which sanctify injustice?
Is it an English law, to rob the weak,
To wring his pittance from the shiv'ring poor,
To levy taxes like a Russian czar,
To stop the course of justice, and let fly
The fiery banners of destructive war,
Of martial law o'er the devoted heads
Of guiltless cities; know you not, good sir,
All laws and usages are made to bend
Before the *magic* influence of an act,
And ordinance of your parliament.

HARMAN.

O then thou'rt angry, that our parliament
Encroaches too much on the king's prerogative;
It has, you think, too great a share of power.

WARREN.

It matters not to us, what power it has
In *England*, whether too little, or too much:
That is *your* care; *look* to it if you're wise:
Your parliament is not ours, nor shall be ours,
Why then presume to legislate for us?
Why dare to levy taxes? that's the question:
'Tis childish to dispute on points of policy,
In which *you* are determin'd, *I* convinc'd.

HARMAN.

O then I see how 'tis, a king displeases you;
You want a commonwealth.

WARREN.

If once the British government's dissolv'd,
We should not choose a monarchy, tho' sway'd
By Trajan or an Antonine; what are kings?
Kings form a horrid junto of conspiracy,
A *Catilinian* compact, 'gainst the lives,
The rights, the peace, the freedom of the world:
They are the Manichean demons, who undo
The good which heaven has done;
They waste with fire
The purple vintage, and the waving grain:

Their butcher hordes they send out to destroy
Themselves, like vultures screaming o'er the field,
Snuff up the blood of armies; horrid sights!
As they appear, young spring her face conceals,
And vegetation shrinks at their approach;
They live by blood, and tears, and sweat, and groans,
They exercise oppression, lust and piracy:
Famine and war, their iron hearted ministers,
Before them go; while prostrate at their feet
Science and freedom, downward to the dust,
Point their dishonor'd faces.

HARMAN.

If these are your opinions, I have done;
Tho' if I might presume to give advice,
You should not slight his excellency's offer;
He will commend you to the royal favor,
And fame and honours will pour fast upon you.

WARREN.

What! then you'd have me be an abject slave,
A sycophant, to follow in his train,
And when he's out of humor — talk to him:
Amuse him with the account of slaughter'd rebels,
Recount his own atchievements in the field,
And close with history of my own apostacy:
'Till at the horrid tale, his furious eyes
Run o'er with brutal joy; young man 'tis well:
Good nature may have prompted you to this.
Now *once for all* my final answer take:

The man you speak to, holds himself as good,
Of as much value as the *man you serve*,
Ay: and of more, while he defends his country,
Than any *pamper'd monarch* on the globe:
All riches and rewards my soul detests,
Which are not earn'd by virtue: I prefer
One hour of life, spent in my country's services,
To ages wasted midst a servile herd
Of *lazy*, *abject*, *fawning*, *cringing* courtiers.
All future business 'twixt your lord and me,
Must be determin'd in the field.

ACT IV.

SCENE — A CHAMBER.

[ELVIRA, *sola.*]

Be still my heart, nor aggravate thy woes:
Mayhap, my letter, wet with new fall'n tears
Back'd by the entreaties of my faithful Anna,
May shake his purpose; shou'd it not, sweet Heaven—
What will become of me: O wretched state!
Bounded by love and duty, who keep watch,
And every ray of hope, that wou'd beam in,
To cheer the joyless prospect of the waste,
Keen as the dragon of th' Hesperides,
They intercept; and leave my soul a night,
So thick and black, that thought doth lose its way.
Anna comes—
Now gracious heaven, support my fainting soul,
And give me strength to hear.
Anna; this face of woe portends no good:
O did you see him?

ANNA.

I did my lady.

ELVIRA.

And into his own hands my letter give?
What said he, did he read it, will he come,
Where did you find him, tell, O tell me all.

ANNA.

Alas my lady, I will tell thee all;
But not one breath of comfort can I give:
Alarm fills the town, and the hoarse note
Of warlike preparation, peals around;
The British troops are sent to storm the post
Of Bunker Hill; I saw them all embark'd,
And steer towards it.

ELVIRA.

O misery! finish, free me from suspense:
Tell me you saw him proudly tread the deck,
Anticipating triumphs o'er this land;
Tell me you saw him tear my foolish note,
And fling it to the winds: while cutting smiles
Of insolent contempt, play'd on his face:
Say that he curs'd me, call'd me doating fool:
Fear not, say all, my soul doth joy to dwell
On kindred horrors.

ANNA.

Ah no —
Cold and distressing as my tidings are,
They do not reach to this; when from the ship,
The gallant youth espy'd me on the shore,

Holding with anxious zeal, thy note aloft:
In agony he clasp'd his hands, and spoke,
I'm sure his lips did move, as if he spoke,
But the big thunder of a hundred guns
Which play'd upon the hill, did drown all sounds,
Save those of its own roaring.

ELVIRA.

Come near me Anna;
My tottering limbs refuse to bear me up:
O thought! O recollection cease forever.
[*Exeunt.* ELVIRA *leaning on* ANNA.]

SCENE II — A VIEW OF BUNKER HILL.

GENERAL WARREN.

[*A view of Sea and Ships.*]

Here am I:
Fix'd on the utmost verge of angry fate,
Which frowning round the summit of this hill,
With threatening gestures, seems to chide my stay.
Yes, Bunker Hill: I view thee as the line,
Which bounds my earthly prospects; as the field,
Which shall enroll me with the mighty dead.
How came I here? not by the stern command
Of any higher power; not dispatch'd,
As forlorn hope, devoted sacrifice,
To take the edge of fury off the foe,
And by my death, to seal an army's safety;

But freely, and of mine own accord,
Have I solicited this arduous post,
To teach my countrymen contempt of death,
To kindle great ideas in their minds:
So Leonidas (I'm vain of the example)
With proud disdain his mighty soul resign'd,
To stem the torrent of invading foes,
Which roar'd upon his country; Godlike man!
And with his little band repress'd the foe;
'Till the proud Persian learnt by thousands slain,
That little Greece, contending for her rights,
Was more than equal to a world in arms.
This hill shall be America's *Thermopylæ;*
Here shall her little band of patriot sons,
Oppose those modern Persians; while the flames
Of smoaking harvests, fir'd at Lexington,
Hairs pluck'd from off the heads of hoary age
By fierce Janizaries, in brutal mirth;
The shrieks of ravish'd matrons, and the cries
Of infants, toss'd upon the ruthless pike;
Shall fill our souls with tenfold fury,
And put a keener edge upon our swords.

[*Two Cannon.*]

Roar on, you hollow ministers of fate—
Fit emblems of the furies, who preside
O'er Britain's councils; we regard you not—
Our cannon shall observe the deepest silence;
But such a silence 'twill be, as exists
In Ætna or Vesuvius; ere they roll
Their scalding lava o'er the works of men:
By and *by*, our answer shall arrive in death,

Borne on the wings of thunder. [*Two Cannon.*]
Double your peals,
Until you burst your throats; you do but use
Our new rais'd soldiers to your surly sounds.
[*Enter* PRESCOTT.]

PRESCOTT.

A soldier comes from Gridly, t'inform us,
That thro' his glass, he can see the foe
Embark, and hither bend their rapid course:
He wants to know, if he shall fire on them
Before they land, or let them disembark,
And unmolested march towards the works.

WARREN.

By all means, let them land:
We wish not to engage at children's play:
When once we meet, the combat shall be mortal,
Let not a gleam or flash inform the foe,
That we await them; keep in dreadful quiet;
Grim as hush'd whirlwinds, or wild beasts in ambush,
That all at once our fire
May bolt upon them, like the wrath of heaven.

PRESCOTT.

I'll take these orders back.

WARREN.

Do not fail
To fan the flame of freedom in the troops:

Tell them their suffering country depends,
Their wives, their children and their aged sires,
On this day's issue; and let the rallying word,
Thro' all the day, be, *Liberty or Death.*

[PRESCOTT *exit.*]

[WARREN *kneels.*]

Now liberty array thee for the fight:
Now from thy proper armoury, draw out
The furious weapons of destructive war.
As thou wast wont, when to Thermopylæ,
Or Salamis, thou led'st thy Grecians out:
Enrobe thy self in *Thunder;* to thy eyes
Add *Lightnings*, to thy visage *wrath:*
Assume the gate of *war*, the whoop of *battle*,
Which hoarsely sounding thro' the burning files
Doth sadden *armies:* then hither fly;
And, with Columbia's new born sons, advance
To raise thy self a temple more superb
Than Rome's proud capitol.

[*Trumpet sounds.*]

This signal summons me away to battle:
Mildness farewell — adieu now soft ey'd pity —

[*Draws his sword.*]

Now savage strife and fury fill my soul —
And when my nature yields to soft compassion
Let Boston's injuries rise before my view,
And steel my heart to pity.

[*Exit.*]

SCENE III — A VIEW OF WATER.

The English are seen passing in boats, to the sound of British musick — they disembark at the foot of Bunker Hill, and form.

PERCY, HOWE, ABERCROMBIE.

PERCY.

'Tis strange, these rebels suffer'd us to land
Without attempting to oppose us.

ABERCROMBIE.

A little time will clear this matter up;
You 'll find they've meaning in it.

HOWE.

Perhaps they have repented of their treason.

ABERCROMBIE.

That, I will last believe.

HOWE.

Have you discover'd who the leader is,
They have entrusted with this enterprize.

PERCY.

A straggler whom we seiz'd without the works,
Declares his name is Warren.

ABERCROMBIE.

That is a name, in high repute among them,
And such a one, these works bespeak the foe,
Rais'd as it were by magic, in a night.

HOWE.

They're truly formidable.
I've reconnoitr'd them, on every side,
And found them so well lin'd with men and cannon,
That to us it appears expedient,
To send to Boston for a reinforcement.

PERCY.

Had we not better see if the supply
Is on its way : what say you Abercrombie ?
Why so dejected man ? does the fair captive
Refuse to be propitious to thy wish ?

ABERCROMBIE.

Hold Percy :
At naming her, my wounds will bleed afresh,
Leave me behind, look you out the supply :

HOWE.

Look close, toward the foe, lest ere supplies arrive,
They meditate a sally.

Exeunt. P. *and* HOWE.
[*Manet* ABERCROMBIE.]

ABERCROMBIE.

Farewell Alvira;
Thy lover bids adieu to thy dear image.
Perhaps the various fortunes of this day.
May shut these eyes forever on thy sight;
Grieve not for me,
If fame should bear the tidings of my fall:
Tho' angry fate forbids us to unite,
Here on the earth; yet in the realms above,
Where threat'ning tyrants and their ministers
Forever are shut out; we 'll meet again.
Curse on the authors of all war and strife:
They are, who fill the world with wretchedness;
Who tread on honor and humanity:
Who rend all ties, which knit the soul together:
E'en love, the solace of the human race,
Their phrenzy spares not.

END OF THE FOURTH ACT.

ACT V.

BUNKER HILL FORTIFIED — DISTANT VIEW OF SEA AND SHIPS.

English reinforced, march towards the Hill. The cannon play at intervals to make breaches in the works. English bands strike up Yankee Doodle in contempt of the Americans. A dead silence reigns among the Americans. They are seen just appearing above the works, waiting the attack. Three times the English make the assault, and three times they are beat back. After the third repulse WARREN *half descends the Hill, and addresses his soldiers :*

Courage, Americans !
The spirits of those heroes, who expir'd
Massacred at Boston and at Lexington,
Are this day witnesses of your renown ;
Suspended o'er this hill; let them behold
Vengeance inflicted on their murderers :
Let's give them in their names another fire,
And in their ears shout, LIBERTY OR DEATH.

[*Americans shout.*]

English again advance, and are again beat back. WARREN *descends the Hill with his Soldiers.*

WARREN.

Heroes retire; this day you've done your part:
To-morrow we will take another post,
And inch by inch contest it with the foe,
If every trifling hill be so ennobled,
In our vast Continent's Geography;
Columbia may with Rome hold up her head,
And move along with empires — Retreat
Brothers, in danger as in victory;
This glorious spot myself the last will leave;
Prescott bring off the troops.

PRESCOTT.

You must not stay behind.

WARREN.

I will not stir till every soul be safe,
Who fought with me this day.

Here a shot comes from the opposite wing, which mortally wounds WARREN. *He falls into the arms of a Grenadier. The English advance. The battle is renewed by the efforts of the Americans to carry off their general. Americans retire.*

FIELD OF BATTLE.

HOWE, PERCY.

HOWE.

This is a melancholy scene of triumph;
Our bravest troops and soldiers strew the plain.

PERCY.

I'm griev'd to know it;
We have a melancholy list to send to England
With kill'd and wounded fill'd:
There's Abercrombie dead, and valiant Pitcairn,
With hundred other souls of generous stamp,
Exclusive of those mountain heaps of slain,
Which baffle calculation.

HOWE.

How many of the foe, in your opinion,
Have we dispatched?

PERCY.

They've left but thirty of their dead behind.

HOWE.

We've lost our bravest troops; and in return,
Have gain'd a paltry hill—This is defeat;

And will be construed so in England:
Who would have thought the rebels would have dar'd
To fire on us?

PERCY.

I knew they would.
Since the first settling of the northern states,
The revolution principles are held
In high esteem; and with the parent state
The Colonists oft wag'd rebellious fight.
What females these? Elvira and her maid!

ELVIRA *is seen coming in preceded, by* ANNA; *her hair loose; her bosom disordered; her eyes wild and haggard.*

The news of Abercrombie's death has reach'd her ears,
And she is come to seek his mangled corpse.

ANNA.

O sirs, my lady is beside herself;
Her lover's death, soon as it reach'd her ears
Depriv'd her of her senses. See her air.
Listen, hear her raving.

ELVIRA.

They stuck him round with arrows,
And flung his lovely corpse upon the shore.

ANNA.

God's mercy on her.

ELVIRA.

Wolves, do not tear him thus.

ANNA.

O heaven, have pity on her.

ELVIRA.

I do not aim at him, my countrymen;
'Twas all my fault.

HOWE.

Sweet lady, let us lead thee from this place.

ELVIRA.

O Abercrombie, love, sweet love, dear love.

PERCY.

Sweet lady, be prevail'd on to retire.

ELVIRA.

Who are you? did *you* kill all these
Poor soldiers? look in my face — ha! there's
Guilt in those eyes — if you kill me, do
Not expose my body with those wretched
Carcases — are you sure they are dead!

[*Treads softly.*]

Hard hearted men, will
You let them die, without assistance!
Soldiers of kings, O spare my gentle father;
Here on my knees, O grant me his sweet life.

HOWE.

Sweet lady, do not fear, we will not hurt thee.

ELVIRA.

Are you not English soldiers?

PERCY.

We are men of honor, lady.

ELVIRA.

Ah, it may be; Abercrombie was an Englishman.
My harden'd heart will burst, I cannot weep—
O Abercrombie, love, sweet love, dear love.
[*Falls faint, on the body of* ABERCROMBIE.]

HOWE.

She faints:
And tired nature gives the struggle up.
Let us convey her from this horrid scene;
Lest when the light revisit her sad eyes,
This scene of slaughter and her lover's blood
May root her Phrenzy so, that it will live,
As long as life. [*They bear her off.*]

Scene changes to another part of the hill. WARREN, *mortally wounded, is borne in by a Grenadier.*

WARREN.

Here lay me down:
That I may take one sad, one farewell look
Of this beloved land; [*Soldier lays him down.*]

My short career of glory soon is run;
But I have fall'n according to my wish:
Fighting amidst my countrymen in arms.
'Tis true, the foe are masters of the field:
But 'tis a slaughter house, fill'd with their dead;
A spectacle, to wring their flinty hearts,
And make them cautious, how they rouse the brave.
This day, has been a proud one for the land:
My countrymen have fought with Spartan valour,
Like hungry lions, bathing them in blood,
And like the Romans, in their first encounter
With Epire's king; have but resign'd the field,
A wretched solace to the mourning foe,
Who in such triumphs sees his strength decay.
My soul now flutters on the wing, to leave
Its earthly mansion, and aspires to live
With Brutus, and the virtuous souls immortal!
I had but *one poor life*, to give my country:
Had I ten thousand, it should have them all.

[*Pauses through weakness.*]

O might I look into the womb of time
And see my country's future destiny:
Cou'd I but see her proud democracy,
Founded on equal laws, and stript entire,
Of those unnatural titles, and those names
Of *King*, of *Count*, of *Stadtholder*, and *Duke*,
Which, with *degrading awe*, possess the world:
My cheered soul, would gather life anew,
And parting from my body, as the dove
Sails from her nest, would singing soar to heaven.

[*To the Soldier.*]

I see that thou art mov'd, good friend;
Heaven will reward thee, for thy pious care,
In bearing from the carnage of this day,
Thy wounded General; consult thy safety:
Nor vainly strive to save a dying man —
The foe's at hand. [*Drums beat.*]

SOLDIER.

I'm not afraid of death sir;
I will defend your person to the last:
Where can I hope to die more gloriously
Than in defence of my belov'd commander?

WARREN.

Thy general orders thee to fly from hence:
Would'st thou deprive thy country of thy service,
When she doth so much need it? go my friend,
And lend thy aid, to crush the savage foe.
Tell the world, 'tis all I ask of thee,
The patriot Warren died without a groan:
That, smiling, midst the agonies of death,
His darling country occupied his thoughts:
That he enjoin'd his sorrowing kindred
To render thanks to the great God of freedom,
That Warren did his duty: — leave me now.
America — my country! bless thee heaven.
O God protect this land — I faint — I die.
Live the Republic. Live; O live, forever.

Scene changes to the American camp. American army moves slowly to the sound of solemn music. Second, the troops out of uniform, who fought on the hill. Third. Children bearing flowers. Fourth. The Bier is brought in, on one side PRESCOTT, *on the other* PUTNAM, *at proper intervals, the standards decorated with republican emblems, and popular devices.*

First standard, ... THE RIGHTS OF MAN.
Second . . . . LIBERTY AND EQUALITY.
Third . . . . HE DIED FOR HIS COUNTRY.
Fourth . . BOSTON, PARENT OF THE REVOLUTION.
Fifth . . . . HATRED TO ROYALTY.
Sixth . . . . A FEDERAL CONSTITUTION.

The Bier is laid down.— Two virgins advance to it, and leaning over it, sing—

[TUNE, ROSLIN CASTLE.]

He dy'd for his country — rain our tears,
His death has banish'd all our fears;
You daughters of Columbia mourn,
With tresses loose, and hearts forlorn:
Amidst the heaps of British slain,
Thy Warren's body strews the plain;
His precious blood was shed for you,
O let us shed our tears in lieu.

When Britain's tyrant, o'er the waves,
Had sent *his* slaves, to make *you* slaves,
Thy gallant Warren, fearless stood,
And dar'd the angry torrent's flood.

Pale with affright, the foe retires,
Swift as he hurls Columbia's fires:
But now he's gone, his spirit flies
From earth, and seeks its kindred skies.

You sons and daughters of the land,
From *all* his virtues tears demand,
You soldiers and you farmers, hear
Your hero's glories with a tear.
And you of Boston, who have seen
Oft in your streets his warlike mien,
Join in the general song of grief,
Which freedom gives to freedom's chief.

Curtain drops slowly. Solemn Dirge.

FINIS.